Albert Einstein

Albert Einstein was a German-born theoretical physicist, widely acknowledged to be one of the greatest physicists of all time. Einstein is best known for developing the theory of relativity, but he also made important contributions to the development of the theory of quantum mechanics.

Born: March 14, 1879, Ulm, Kingdom of Württemberg, German Empire

Died: April 18, 1955, Princeton, New Jersey, U.S

Children: Eduard Einstein, Hans Albert Einstein, Lieserl Einstein

Spouse: Elsa Einstein (m. 1919–1936), Mileva Marić (m. 1903–1919)

Education: University of Zurich (1905), ETH Zürich (1896–1900

Parents: Hermann Einstein, Pauline Einstein

Early correspondence between Einstein and Marić was discovered and published in 1987 which revealed that the couple had a daughter named "Lieserl", born in early 1902 in Novi Sad where Marić was staying with her parents. Marić returned to Switzerland without the child, whose real name and fate are unknown.

After graduating in 1900, Einstein spent almost two frustrating years searching for a teaching post. He acquired Swiss citizenship in February 1901 but was not conscripted for medical reasons. With the help of Marcel Grossmann's father, he secured a job in Bern at the Swiss Patent Office, as an assistant examiner.

Einstein evaluated patent applications for a variety of devices including a gravel sorter and an electromechanical typewriter. In 1903, his position at the Swiss Patent Office became permanent, although he was passed over for promotion until he "fully mastered machine technology"

By 1908, he was recognized as a leading scientist and was appointed lecturer at the University of Bern. The following year, after he gave a lecture on electrodynamics and the relativity principle at the University of Zurich, Alfred Kleiner recommended him to the faculty for a newly created professorship in theoretical physics. Einstein was appointed associate professor in 1909.

Albert Einstein is well known for his equation $E = mc2$, which argues that energy and mass (matter) are one and the same thing. He is well remembered for discovering the photoelectric effect, for which he was awarded the Nobel Prize in Physics in 1921. Einstein established special and general relativity ideas, which helped to complicate and build upon notions proposed by Isaac Newton more than 200 years before.

Prolific thinker and famous quote creator

The practice of misattributing quotes has been going on for as long as anybody can remember. People prefer to credit statements to famous people that sound like something they might have said but that they didn't actually say once they gain a reputation for saying witty, profound, or inspiring things.

This is a list of 501 quotes from Albert Einstein. The list has no special order.

This is an effort to collect inspiring quotes attributed to Albert Einstein. Certainly, one of them can inspire you.

We hope this collection will Inspire You

Humblepics.com

Quote Collection

Don't wait for miracles, your whole life is a miracle.

Learn from yesterday, live for today, hope for tomorrow. The important thing is not to stop questioning.

The height of stupidity is most clearly demonstrated by the individual who ridicules something he knows nothing about.

Blind belief in authority is the greatest enemy of truth.

Everyone knew it was impossible, until a fool who didn't know came along and did it.

A person who never made a mistake never tried anything new.

Experience is knowledge. All the rest is information.

Thinking is hard work; that's why so few do it.

Failure is success in progress

Three great forces rule the world: stupidity, fear and greed.

Insanity: doing the same thing over and over again and expecting different results.

In the middle of every difficulty lies opportunity.

If you want different results, do not do the same things.

Be a voice not an echo.

You can't use an old map to explore a new world.

If you want to live a happy life, tie it to a goal, not to people or objects.

Only two things are infinite, the universe and human stupidity, and I'm not sure about the former.

Strive not to be a success, but rather to be of value.

A clever person solves a problem. A wise person avoids it.

Intelligence is not the ability to store information, but to know where to find it.

Genius is 1% talent and 99% percent hard work.

There comes a point in your life when you need to stop reading other people's books and write your own.

Genius is making complex ideas simple, not making simple ideas complex

Any fool can know. The point is to understand.

I'm more interested in the future than in the past, because the future is where I intend to live.

I don't need to know everything, I just need to know where to find it, when I need it

Don't let your brain interfere with your heart.

We cannot get to where we dream of being tomorrow unless we change our thinking today.

Success = 1 part work + 1 part play + 1 part keep your mouth shut

Never do anything against conscience even if the state demands it.

If one day you have to choose between the world and love, remember this: If you choose the world you'll be left without love, but if you choose love, with it you will conquer the world

Knowledge and ego are directly related. the less knowledge, the greater the ego

You never fail until you stop trying.

Creativity is seeing what others see and thinking what no one else has ever thought.

A ship is always safe at the shore - but that is NOT what it is built for.

God did not create evil. Just as darkness is the absence of light, evil is the absence of God.

Once you stop learning, you start dying

Condemnation before investigation is the highest form of ignorance.

Men marry women with the hope they will never change. Women marry men with the hope they will change. Invariably they are both disappointed.

Three Rules of Work: Out of clutter find simplicity. From discord find harmony. In the middle of difficulty lies opportunity.

The true sign of intelligence is not knowledge but imagination.

Make everything as simple as possible, but not simpler.

There is a driving force more powerful than steam, electricity and nuclear power: the will.

I have only two rules which I regard as principles of conduct. The first is: Have no rules. The second is: Be independent of the opinion of others.

Coincidence is God's way of remaining anonymous.

The Press, which is mostly controlled by vested interests, has an excessive influence on public opinion.

I must be willing to give up what I am in order to become what I will be.

When the solution is simple, God is answering.

You do not really understand something unless you can explain it to your grandmother.

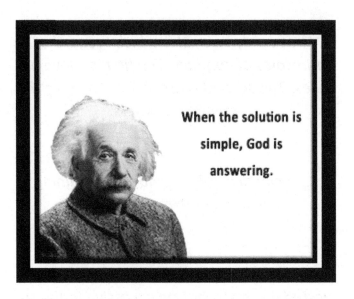

If the bee disappeared off the surface of the globe, then man would have only four years of life left. No more bees, no more pollination, no more plants, no more animals, no more man.

The mind that opens to a new idea never returns to its original size

How many people are trapped in their everyday habits: part numb, part frightened, part indifferent? To have a better life we must keep choosing how we are living.

At least once a day, allow yourself the freedom to think and dream for yourself.

Peace cannot be kept by force; it can only be achieved by understanding.

Most people see what is, and never see what can be.

The true definition of madness is repeating the same action, over and over, hoping for a different result.

Live with purpose. Don't let people or things around you get you down.

When you sit with a nice girl for two hours, it seems like two minutes; when you sit on a hot stove for two minutes, it seems like two hours. That's relativity.

Nothing happens unless something moves.

I'd rather be an optimist and a fool than a pessimist and right.

Creativity is intelligence having fun.

I am neither especially clever nor especially gifted. I am only very, very curious.

Never underestimate your own ignorance.

Don't listen to their words, fix your attention on their deeds.

I refuse to engage in an intellectual battle with an unarmed man.

Persistence is the most powerful force on earth, it can move mountains.

The intuitive mind is a sacred gift and the rational mind is a faithful servant. We have created a society that honors the servant and has forgotten the gift.

If A is a success in life, then A equals x plus y plus z. Work is x; y is play; and z is keeping your mouth shut

The more I learn, the more I realize I don't know.

If I had only one hour to save the world, I would spend fifty-five minutes defining the problem, and only five minutes finding the solution.

Imagination is more important than knowledge. Knowledge is limited. Imagination encircles the world.

I believe we are here to do good. It is the responsibility of every human being to aspire to do something worthwhile, to make the world a better place than the one we found.

Adversity introduces a man to himself.

Student is not a container you have to fill but a torch you have to light up.

A bartender is just a pharmacist with a limited inventory.

Stupidity is a personal achievement which transcends national boundaries.

A great thought begins by seeing something differently, with a shift of the mind's eye.

The best design is the simplest one that works.

The ideas that have lighted my way have been kindness, beauty and truth.

The world is in greater peril from those who tolerate or encourage evil than from those who actually commit it.

Energy cannot be created or destroyed, it can only be changed from one form to another.

No problem can be solved from the same level of consciousness that created it.

Those who have the privilege to know have the duty to act.

Logic will get you from A to B. Imagination will take you everywhere.

The only mistake in life is the lesson not learned.

The world is a dangerous place to live; not because of the people who are evil, but because of the people who don't do anything about it.

Do not grow old, no matter how long you live. Never cease to stand like curious children before the Great Mystery into which we were born.

Many of the things you can count, don't count. Many of the things you can't count, really count.

Know where to find the information and how to use it - That's the secret of success.

I have made the Bhagwad Gita as the main source of my inspiration and guide for the purpose of scientific investigations and formation of my theories.

It may be possible to fight intolerance, stupidity, and fanaticism separately, but when they come together there is no hope.

When you trip over love, it is easy to get up. But when you fall in love, it is impossible to stand again.

Be kind to people who are different from you.

Compound interest is the eighth wonder of the world. He who understands it, earns it ... he who doesn't ... pays it.

It is the supreme art of the teacher to awaken joy in creative expression and knowledge.

It is entirely possible that behind the perception of our senses, worlds are hidden of which we are unaware.

If you can't explain what you are doing to a nine-year-old, then either you still don't understand it very well, or it's not all that worthwhile in the first place.

The person with big dreams is more powerful than one with all the facts.

It would seem that men always need some idiotic fiction in the name of which they can hate one another. Once it was religion. Now it is the State.

Matter is Energy ... Energy is Light ... We are all Light Beings

There is a race between mankind and the universe. Mankind is trying to build bigger, better, faster, and more foolproof machines. The universe is trying to build bigger, better, and faster fools. So far the universe is winning.

I came to America because of the great, great freedom which I heard existed in this country. I made a mistake in selecting America as a land of freedom, a mistake I cannot repair in the balance of my lifetime.

Time is not at all what it seems. It does not flow in only one direction, and the future exists simultaneously with the past.

Outer changes always begin with an inner change of attitude.

Highly developed spirits often encounter resistance from mediocre minds.

Everyone should be respected as an individual, but no one idolized.

Even if you have to go through hell - go without hesitation.

You have to learn the rules of the game. And then you have to play better than anyone else.

Remember today, for it is the beginning of always. Today marks the start of a brave new future filled with all your dreams can hold. Think truly to the future and make those dreams come true.

If at first the idea is not absurd, then there is no hope for it.

Never memorize what you can look up in a book.

People like us, who believe in physics, know that the distinction between past, present, and future is only a stubbornly persistent illusion.

Imagination is more important than knowledge.

If I were not a physicist, I would probably be a musician. I often think in music. I live my daydreams in music. I see my life in terms of music.

Try first to be a man of value; success will follow.

Even a fool is wise after an event.

The minority, the ruling class at present, has the schools and press, usually the Church as well, under its thumb. This enables it to organize and sway the emotions of the masses, and make its tool of them.

More the knowledge lesser the Ego, lesser the knowledge, more the Ego.

Compassionate people are geniuses in the art of living, more necessary to the dignity, security, and joy of humanity than the discoverers of knowledge.

If you want to know the future, look at the past.

The individual who has experienced solitude will not easily become a victim of mass suggestion.

Condemnation without investigation is the height of ignorance

Our task must be to free ourselves by widening our circle of compassion to embrace all living creatures and the whole of nature and its beauty.

Education is what remains after one has forgotten what one has learned in school.

All conditions and all circumstances in our lives are a result of a certain level of thinking. If we want to change the conditions and circumstances, we have to change the level of thinking that is responsible for it.

The most important thing is to not stop questioning.

If you can't explain something simply, you don't know enough about it.

To be free means to be independent, not to be influenced by what others think and say.

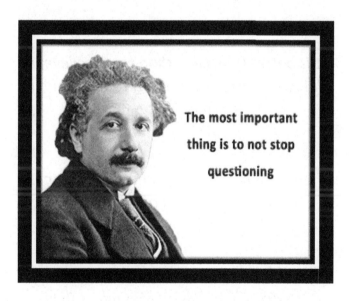

The state is made for man, not man for the state.... That is to say, the state should be our servant and not we its slaves

I never allow myself to become discouraged under any circumstances. The three great essentials to achieve anything worthwhile are first, hard work, second, stick-to- stick-to-it-iveness, third, common sense.

When I read the Bhagavad-Gita and reflect about how God created this universe everything else seems so superfluous

It is better to believe than to disbelieve; in doing you bring everything to the realm of possibility.

There is only one road to human greatness: through the school of hard knocks.

When I have one week to solve a seemingly impossible problem, I spend six days defining the problem. Then, the solution becomes obvious.

Concerning matter, we have been all wrong. What we have called matter is energy, whose vibration has been so lowered as to be perceptible to the senses. There is no matter.

The value of a college education is not the learning of many facts but the training of the mind to think

Those who manage their way into a crisis are not necessarily the right people to manage their way out of a crisis

The dog is very smart. He feels sorry for me because I receive so much mail; that's why he tries to bite the mailman.

The only thing we can be certain of in this life is that we can be certain of nothing.

Out of clutter, find simplicity.

Solitude is painful when one is young, but delightful when one is more mature.

One should not pursue goals that are easily achieved. One must develop an instinct for what one can just barely achieve through one's greatest efforts.

The world is not threatened by evil people, but by those who allow evil to take place.

To obtain an assured favorable response from people, it is better to offer them something for their stomachs instead of their brains.

Once we accept our limits, we go beyond them.

Genius abhors consensus because when consensus is reached, thinking stops. Stop nodding your head.

God reveals himself in the orderly harmony of what exists.

Whoever is careless with the truth in small matters cannot be trusted in important affairs.

We can understand almost anything, but we can't understand how we understand.

Look deep into nature, and then you will understand everything better.

I admit that thoughts influence the body.

Life is a preparation for the future; and the best preparation for the future is to live as if there were none.

Truth is what stands the test of experience.

The thinking that got us to where we are is not the thinking that will get us to where we want to be.

Have the courage to take your own thoughts seriously, for they will shape you.

If we knew what it was we were doing, it would not be called research, would it?

Paper is to write things down that we need to remember. Our brains are used to think.

The only justifiable purpose of political institutions is to ensure the unhindered development of the individual.

The devil has put a penalty on all things we enjoy in life. Either we suffer in our health, or we suffer in our soul, or we get fat.

Never regard study as a duty, but as the enviable opportunity to learn

If someone feels that he has never made a mistake in his life, it only means that he has never tried anything new in his life.

It's not that I'm so smart, it's just that I stay with problems longer.

It takes a touch of genius - and a lot of courage to move in the opposite direction.

Science without religion is lame, religion without science is blind.

Where there is love, there is no imposition.

Earth is the insane asylum of the universe.

The only source of knowledge is experience.

There's no question dolphins are smarter than humans as they play more.

I believe in intuitions and inspirations...I sometimes FEEL that I am right. I do not KNOW that I am.

I think 99 times and find nothing. I stop thinking, swim in the silence, and the truth comes to me.

When you examine the lives of the most influential people who have ever walked among us, you discover one thread that winds through them all. They have been aligned first with their spiritual nature and only then with their physical selves.

The important things are always simple.

The intellect has little to do on the road to discovery. There comes a leap in consciousness, call it Intuition or what you will, the solution comes to you and you don't know how or why.

Future medicine will be the medicine of frequencies.

There's a genius in all of us.

Everyone has two choices. We're either full of love... or full of fear.

Racism is America's greatest disease, racism is a disease of the white man.

Everything you can imagine, nature has already created.

I never think of the future - it comes soon enough.

Education is not received. It is achieved.

Past is dead Future is uncertain; Present is all you have, So eat, drink and live merry.

Matter is spirit reduced to point of visibility.

Imagination is the highest form of research.

All that's different about me is that I still ask the questions most people stopped asking at age five.

Life isn't worth living, unless it is lived for someone else.

Imagination is vastly more important than intelligence.

Our separation from each other is an optical illusion.

I am content in my later years. I have kept my good humor and take neither myself nor the next person seriously.

Nothing causes more consternation in a group of hypocrites than one honest man.

Scientists investigate that which already is; Engineers create that which has never been.

We act as though comfort and luxury were the chief requirements of life. All that we need to make us happy is something to be enthusiastic about.

I don't teach my students, I provide the circumstances in which they can learn.

The tragedy of life is what dies in the hearts and souls of people while they live.

One should never impose one's views on a problem; one should rather study it, and in time a solution will reveal itself.

If you have never failed, you have never tried anything new.

Real sign of intelligence isn't knowledge, it's imagination

I speak to everyone in the same way, whether he is the garbage man or the president of the university.

I live in that solitude which is painful in youth, but delicious in the years of maturity.

Education is only a ladder to gather fruit from the tree of knowledge, not the fruit itself

Albert is a very poor student. He is mentally slow, unsociable and is always daydreaming. He is spoiling it for the rest of the class. It would be in the best interests of all if he were removed from school immediately.

The truth of a theory can never be proven, for one never knows if future experience will contradict its conclusions.

I love Humanity but I hate humans

Learning is experience. Everything else is just information.

The greater the doubt, the greater the awakening

The most precious things in life are not those you get for money.

Every day I remind myself that my inner and outer life are based on the labors of other men, living and dead, and that I must exert myself in order to give in the same measure as I have received and am still receiving.

Peace comes through understanding

The main task of the spirit is to free man from his ego.

If I had an hour to solve a problem I'd spend 55 minutes thinking about the problem and 5 minutes thinking about solutions.

A thought that sometimes makes me hazy: Am I - or are the others crazy?

Example isn't another way to teach, it is the only way to teach.

It has become appallingly obvious that our technology has exceeded our humanity.

The only race I know is the human one.

A society's competitive advantage will come not from how well its schools teach the multiplication and periodic tables, but from how well they stimulate imagination and creativity.

We dance for laughter, we dance for tears, we dance for madness, we dance for fears, we dance for hopes, we dance for screams, we are the dancers, we create the dreams.

The true measure of a man is the degree to which he has managed to subjugate his ego.

To act intelligently in human affairs is only possible if an attempt is made to understand the thoughts, motives, and apprehension of one's opponent so fully that one can see the world through their eyes.

The most important human endeavor is the striving for morality in our actions. Our inner balance and even our very existence depend on it. Only morality in our actions can give beauty and dignity to life.

Philosophy is empty if it isn't based on science. Science discovers, philosophy interprets.

Life is a great tapestry. The individual is only an insignificant thread in an immense and miraculous pattern.

Great spirits have always encountered violent opposition from mediocre minds.

If the facts don't fit the theory, change the facts.

The stupid are invincible.

What a sad era when it is easier to smash an atom than a prejudice.

The human spirit must prevail over technology.

Men should continue to fight, but they should fight for things worth while, not for imaginary geographical lines, racial prejudices and private greed draped in the color's of patriotism.

The monotony and solitude of a quiet life stimulates the creative mind.

Most people say that it is the intellect which makes a great scientist. They are wrong: it is character.

The value of achievement lies in the achieving.

Love is a better teacher than duty.

I have no special talent. I am only passionately curious. The important thing is to not stop questioning. Curiosity has its own reason for existing.

That is the way to learn the most, that when you are doing something with such enjoyment that you don't notice that the time passes.

Nothing will benefit human health and increase the chances for survival of life on Earth as much as the evolution to a vegetarian diet.

Our lives will be measured by what we do for others

We will never be able to solve the problems of tomorrow with the thinking of today

The intuitive mind is a sacred gift.

Bureaucracy is the death of all sound work.

The thing is, not to stop questioning.

Striving for social justice is the most valuable thing to do in life.

The economic anarchy of capitalist society as it exists today is, in my opinion, the real source of evil.

In order to be an immaculate member of a flock of sheep, one must above all be a sheep oneself.

Every one who is seriously involved in the pursuit of science becomes convinced that a spirit is manifest in the laws of the Universe-a spirit vastly superior to that of man, and one in the face of which we with our modest powers must feel humble.

You might as well not be alive if you're not in awe of God.

We can't solve today's problems with the mentality that created them.

An expert is a person who has few new ideas; a beginner is a person with many.

My mind is my laboratory.

If people would only talk about what they understood, Earth would be a very quiet place.

The important thing is to never stop questioning. Never lose a holy curiosity.

A true genius admits that he/she knows nothing.

If you feed your mind as often as you feed your stomach, then you'll never have to worry about feeding your stomach or a roof over your head or clothes on your back.

There are two ways to live: you can live as if nothing is a miracle; you can live as if everything is a miracle.

Creativity is contagious. Pass it on.

In matters of truth and justice, there is no difference between large and small problems, for issues concerning the treatment of people are all the same.

A man must learn to understand the motives of human beings, their illusions, and their sufferings.

It is only to the individual that a soul is given.

While I am a convinced pacifist there are circumstances in which I believe the use of force is appropriate - namely, in the face of an enemy unconditionally bent on destroying me and my people.

Human beings can attain a worthy and harmonious life only if they are able to rid themselves, within the limits of human nature, of the striving for the wish fulfillment of material kinds. The goal is to raise the spiritual values of society.

Nothing happens until something moves.

There two things that are infinite, human stupidity and the universe, I don't know about the universe

Any society which does not insist upon respect for all life must necessarily decay.

The more I learn of physics, the more I am drawn to metaphysics.

Art is standing with one hand extended into the universe and one hand extended into the world, and letting ourselves be a conduit for passing energy.

An oligarchy of private capital cannot be effectively checked even by a democratically organized political society because under existing conditions, private capitalists inevitably control, directly or indirectly, the main sources of information.

All meaningful and lasting change starts first in your imagination and then works its way out. Imagination is more important than knowledge.

I never made one of my discoveries through the process of rational thinking

One should respect an honest person even if he expresses opinions differing from one's own.

Body and soul are not two different things, but only two different ways of perceiving the same thing. Similarly, physics and psychology are only different attempts to link our experiences together by way of systematic thought.

That deep emotional conviction of the presence of a superior reasoning power, which is revealed in the incomprehensible universe, forms my idea of God.

Although I am a typical loner in my daily life, my awareness of belonging to the invisible community of those who strive for truth, beauty, and justice has prevented me from feelings of isolation.

I want to know how God created this world. I am not interested in this or that phenomenon, in the spectrum of this or that element. I want to know God's thoughts, the rest are details.

It is abhorrent to me when a fine intelligence is paired with an unsavory character.

The Universe is stranger than we imagine!

Politics is a pendulum whose swings between anarchy and tyranny are fueled by perennially rejuvenated illusions.

Live your life... as though everything is a miracle.

Experts are just trained dogs.

Everything that is really great and inspiring is created by the individual who can labor in freedom.

My feeling is religious insofar as I am imbued with the consciousness of the insufficiency of the human mind to understand more deeply the harmony of the Universe which we try to formulate as "laws of nature".

It is harder to crack prejudice than an atom.

Only morality in our actions can give beauty and dignity to life.

I have yet to meet a single person from our culture, no matter what his or her educational background, IQ, and specific training, who had powerful transpersonal experiences and continues to subscribe to the materialistic monism of Western science.

I live my daydreams in music I see my life in terms of music. I get most joy in life out of music.

Mozart's music is so pure and beautiful that I see it as a reflection of the inner beauty of the universe.

Once you stop learning, you start dying

Reading, after a certain age, diverts the mind too much from its creative pursuits. Any man who reads too much and uses his own brain too little falls into lazy habits of thinking.

The more cruel the wrong that men commit against an individual or a people, the deeper their hatred and contempt for their victim.

I am a deeply religious nonbeliever - this is a somewhat new kind of religion.

Force always attracts men of low morality.

Given the millions of billions of Earth-like planets, life elsewhere in the Universe without a doubt, does exist. In the vastness of the Universe we are not alone.

Our death is not an end if we can live on in our children and the younger generation. For they are us; our bodies are only wilted leaves on the tree of life.

Arrows of hate have been aimed at me too, but they have never hit me, because somehow they belonged to another world with which I have no connection whatsoever.

A perfection of means, and confusion of aims, seems to be our main problem.

Enjoying the joys of others and suffering with them-these are the best guides for man.

So I stopped wearing socks.

Memory is deceptive because it is colored by today's events.

Learn from yesterday, live for today.

You can't blame gravity for falling in love.

All of us who are concerned for peace and triumph of reason and justice must be keenly aware how small an influence reason and honest good will exert upon events in the political field.

Everything what's inspiring has been created by one who could work in freedom

Games are the most elevated form of investigation.

It is a miracle that curiosity survives formal education.

Indeed, it is not intellect, but intuition which advances humanity. Intuition tells man his purpose in this life.

The high destiny of the individual is to serve rather than to rule.

A scientist is a mimosa when he himself has made a mistake, and a roaring lion when he discovers a mistake of others.

Imagination is everything. It is the preview of life's coming attractions.

Anyone who doesn't take truth seriously in small matters cannot be trusted in large ones either.

Be a loner. That gives you time to wonder.

Everything is energy and that's all there is to it.

Vegetarian food leaves a deep impression on our nature. If the whole world adopts vegetarianism, it can change the destiny of humankind.

I never teach my pupils, I only attempt to provide the conditions in which they can learn.

It is difficult to say what truth is, but sometimes it is so easy to recognize a falsehood.

The true value of a human being can be found in the degree to which he has attained liberation from the self.

Time and space are not conditions of existence, time and space is a model for thinking

No amount of experimentation can ever prove me right; a single experiment can prove me wrong.

An empty stomach is not a good political adviser.

I know not with what weapons World War III will be fought, but World War IV will be fought with sticks and stones.

Any man who can drive safely while kissing a pretty girl is simply not giving the kiss the attention it deserves.

Never lose a holy curiosity. Try not to become a man of success but rather try to become a man of value. He is considered successful in our day who gets more out of life than he puts in. But a man of value will give more than he receives.

We have to do the best we are capable of. This is our sacred human responsibility.

Imagination is more powerful than knowledge.

Please explain the problem to me slowly, as I do not understand things quickly.

The real problem is in the hearts and minds of men. It is not a problem of physics but of ethics. It is easier to denature plutonium than to denature the evil spirit of man.

Don't become a seeker of success. Become a person of value.

A life directed chiefly toward the fulfillment of personal desires will sooner or later always lead to bitter disappointment.

Small is the number of them that see with their own eyes and feel with their own hearts.

We owe a lot to the Indians, who taught us how to count, without which no worthwhile scientific discovery could have been made.

It is every man's obligation to put back into the world at least the equivalent of what he takes out of it.

Do not worry about your difficulties in Mathematics. I can assure you mine are still greater.

The only sure way to avoid making mistakes is to have no new ideas.

Dostoevsky gives me more than any scientist, more than Gauss.

Weakness of attitude becomes weakness of character.

The value of a man resides in what he gives

If people are good because they fear punishment, and hope for reward, then we are a sorry lot indeed.

The one who walks alone, is likely to find himself in places no one has ever been.

Teaching should be such that what is offered is perceived as a valuable gift and not as a hard duty.

Nothing truly valuable can be achieved except by the unselfish cooperation of many individuals.

Time and space are modes by which we think and not conditions in which we live.

I wish to do something Great and Wonderful, but I must start by doing the little things like they were Great and Wonderful

In a healthy nation there is a kind of dramatic balance between the will of the people and the government, which prevents its degeneration into tyranny.

Life is sacred, that is to say, it is the supreme value, to which all other values are subordinate.

The most beautiful thing we can experience is the mysterious. It is the source of all true art and science.

Since our inner experiences consist of reproductions, and combinations of sensory impressions, the concept of a soul without a body seem to me to be empty and devoid of meaning.

Don't dream of being a good person, be a human being is valuable and gives value to life.

When you look at yourself from a universal standpoint, something inside always reminds or informs you that there are bigger and better things to worry about.

The most beautiful gift of nature is that it gives one pleasure to look around and try to comprehend what we see.

The world as we have created it is a process of our thinking. It cannot be changed without changing our thinking.

With fame I become more and more stupid, which of course is a very common phenomenon.

A man should look for what is, and not for what he thinks should be.

The only thing that interferes with my learning is my education.

I learned many years ago never to waste time trying to convince my colleagues.

Intellectual growth should commence at birth and cease only at death.

The definition of genius is taking the complex and making it simple.

God is clever, but not dishonest.

Necessity is the mother of all invention.

The most important decision we make is whether we believe we live in a friendly or hostile universe.

When a man is sufficiently motivated, discipline will take care of itself.

The chicken did not cross the road. The road passed beneath the chicken.

Feeling and longing are the motive forces behind all human endeavor and human creations.

If you do the same thing over and over again you cannot ever expect a different outcome.

It's not that life has been easy, perfect or exactly as expected. I just choose to be happy and grateful no matter how it all turns out. If people are good only because they fear punishment, and hope for reward, then we are a sorry lot indeed.

In a sailboat I become oblivious to everything else in the world.

Here's a Challenge: Study a complicated topic in such detail that anyone interested can nod their head and understand as you explain specific concepts within the topic.

A happy man is too satisfied with the present to dwell too much on the future.

The religion of the future will be a cosmic religion. The religion which based on experience, which refuses dogmatic. If there's any religion that would cope the scientific needs it will be Buddhism.

The future is of greater interest to me than the past, since that is where I intend to spend the rest of my life.

I hope that someday, our humanity might yet surpass our technology.

Nothing happens until something moves. When something vibrates, the electrons of the entire universe resonate with it. Everything is connected.

God does not play dice.

I am also convinced that one gains the purest joy from spirited things only when they are not tied in with earning one's livelihood.

Conceptions without experience are void; experience without conceptions is blind.

The gift of fantasy has meant more to me than my talent for absorbing positive knowledge.

Imagination without knowledge may create beautiful things, knowledge without imagination can create only perfect ones.

As I have said so many times, God doesn't play dice with the world.

Playfulness is the essential feature of productive thought.

Keep fighting until the last buzzer sounds.

A hundred times every day I remind myself that my inner and outer life are based on the labors of others.

The only real valuable thing is intuition.

Not all that counts, can be counted

Most teachers waste their time by asking question which are intended to discover what a pupil does not know whereas the true art of questioning has for its purpose to discover what pupils knows or is capable of knowing.

Politics is more difficult than physics.

Nothing in the world makes people so afraid as the influence of independent-minded people.

The heart says yes, but the mind says no.

Human beings, vegetables, or cosmic dust, we all dance to a mysterious tune, intoned in the distance by an invisible piper.

I prefer to make up my own quotes and attribute them to very smart people, so that I can use them to win arguments

Physical concepts are free creations of the human mind, and are not, however it may seem, uniquely determined by the external world.

That which is impenetrable to us really exists. Behind the secrets of nature remains something subtle, intangible, and inexplicable. Veneration for this force beyond anything that we can comprehend is my religion.

To raise new questions, new possibilities, to regard old problems from a new angle, requires creative imagination and marks real advance in science.

Nature conceals her secrets because she is sublime, not because she is a trickster.

Only one who devotes himself to a cause with his whole strength and soul can be a true master. For this reason mastery demands all of a person.

Creative energy is more critical than learning.

I believe in standardizing automobiles. I do not believe in standardizing human beings. Standardization is a great peril which threatens American culture.

Problems cannot be solved by thinking within the framework in which the problems were created.

It is not a lack of real affection that scares me away again and again from marriage. Is it a fear of the comfortable life, of nice furniture, of dishonor that I burden myself with, or even the fear of becoming a contented bourgeois.

Am I, or the others crazy?

The world we have created is a product of our thinking.

Before God we are all equally wise - and equally foolish.

The leader is one who, out of the clutter, brings simplicity... out of discord, harmony... and out of difficulty, opportunity.

Intellectuals solve problems, geniuses prevent them.

We still do not know one thousandth of one percent of what nature has revealed to us.

I have tried 99 times and have failed, but on the 100th time came success.

True knowledge comes with deep understanding of a topic and its inner workings.

If you are out to describe the truth, leave elegance to the tailor.

God is subtle but he is not malicious.

Genius is when an idea and the execution of that idea are simultaneous.

Nationalism is an infantile disease. It is the measles of mankind.

Only the one who does not question is safe from making a mistake.

The individual must not merely wait and criticize, he must defend the cause the best he can. The fate of the world will be such as the world deserves.

The same thinking that has led you to where you are is not going to lead you to where you want to go.

He who can no longer pause to wonder and stand rapt in awe, is as good as dead; his eyes are closed.

As our circle of knowledge expands, so does the circumference of darkness surrounding it.

I have come to know the mutability of all human relationships and have learned to insulate myself against both heat and cold so that a temperature balance is fairly well assured.

In my experience, the best creative work is never done when one is unhappy.

It almost seems to me that man was not born to be a carnivore.

The pursuit of knowledge for its own sake, an almost fanatical love of justice and the desire for personal independence -- these are the features of the Jewish tradition which make me thank my stars that I belong to it.

Is it not a terrible thing to be forced by society to do things which all of us as individuals regard as abominable crimes?

I want to know all Gods thoughts; all the rest are just details.

Everyone sits in the prison of his own ideas; he must burst it open, and that in his youth, and so try to test his ideas on reality.

I assert that the cosmic religious experience is the strongest and the noblest driving force behind scientific research.

A country cannot simultaneously prepare and prevent war.

I want to be cremated so people won't come to worship at my bones.

There is separation of colored people from white people in the United States. That separation is not a disease of colored people. It is a disease of white people. I do not intend to be quiet about it.

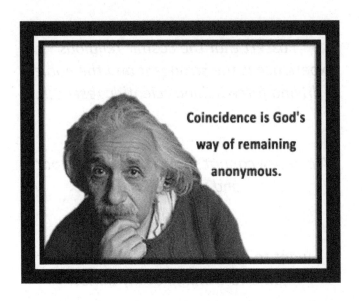

Coincidence is God's way of remaining anonymous.

The led must not be compelled; they must be able to choose their own leader.

Anger dwells only in the bosom of fools.

Empathy is patiently and sincerely seeing the world through the other person's eyes. It is not learned in school; it is cultivated over a lifetime.

Art is the expression of the profoundest thoughts in the simplest way.

My religion consists of a humble admiration of the illimitable superior spirit who reveals himself in the slight details we are able to perceive with our frail and feeble mind.

I never said half the crap people said I did.

Why should I remember anything if I can just look it up?

Imagination is more important than knowledge. For knowledge is limited to all we now know and understand, while imagination embraces the entire world, and all there ever will be to know and understand.

The Bible is a great source of wisdom and consolation and should be read frequently.

Nothing will end war unless the peoples themselves refuse to go to war.

For an idea that does not first seem insane, there is no hope.

The pursuit of truth and beauty is a sphere of activity in which we are permitted to remain children all our lives.

Small is the number of people who see with their eyes and think with their minds.

Matter is real to my senses, but they aren't trustworthy. If Galileo or Copernicus had accepted what they saw, they would never have discovered the movement of the earth and planets.

God is a scientist, not a magician.

My life is a simple thing that would interest no one. It is a known fact that I was born, and that is all that is necessary.

Never lose a holy curiosity.

A person starts to live when he can live outside himself.

Nonsense, seems to sum up everything.

The basic laws of the universe are simple, but because our senses are limited, we can't grasp them. There is a pattern in creation.

I have no particular talent. I am merely inquisitive.

The future is an unknown, but a somewhat predictable unknown. To look to the future we must first look back upon the past. That is where the seeds of the future were planted. I never think of the future. It comes soon enough.

Pure logical thinking cannot yield us any knowledge of the empirical world. All knowledge of reality starts from experience and ends in it.

Women marry men hoping they will change. Men marry women hoping they will not.

If I had an hour to solve a problem and my life depended on the solution, I would spend the first 55 minutes determining the proper question to ask, for once I know the proper question, I could solve the problem in less than five minutes.

Whatever there is of God and goodness in the universe, it must work itself out and express itself through us. We cannot stand aside and let God do it.

But love brings much happiness - much more so than pining brings pain.

The most aggravating thing about the younger generation is that I no longer belong to it.

I have deep faith that the principle of the universe will be beautiful and simple

Compounding is the 8th wonder of the world.

You have to color outside the lines once in a while if you want to make your life a masterpiece.

All I want to do is learn to think like God. All the rest is just details.

For me the Jewish religion like all other religions is an incarnation of the most childish superstitions.

The secret to creativity is knowing how to hide your sources.

I believe, indeed, that overemphasis on the purely intellectual attitude, often directed solely to the practical and factual, in our education, has led directly to the impairment of ethical values.

Long hair minimizes the need for barbers; socks can be done without; one leather jacket solves the coat problem for many years; suspenders are superfluous.

Failure is only postponed success as long as courage 'coaches' ambition.

In theory, theory and practice are the same. In practice, they are not.

It gives me great pleasure indeed to see the stubbornness of an incorrigible nonconformist warmly acclaimed.

When forced to summarize the general theory of relativity in one sentence: Time and space and gravitation have no separate existence from matter.

No problem is ever solved in the same consciousness that was used to create it.

Let every man judge according to his own standards, by what he has himself read, not by what others tell him.

The most powerful force in the world is compound interest.

Every kind of peaceful cooperation among men is primarily based on mutual trust and only secondarily on institutions such as courts of justice and police.

It is a very grave mistake to think that the enjoyment of seeing and searching can be promoted by means of coercion and a sense of duty.

If you're not sure why you're doing something, you can never do enough of it. Imagination is more important than knowledge.

I love to travel, but hate to arrive.

I didn't arrive at my understanding of the fundamental laws of the universe through my rational mind.

I want to go when I want. It is tasteless to prolong life artificially. I have done my share, it is time to go. I will do it elegantly.

Children don't heed the life experiences of their parents, and nations ignore history. Bad lessons always have to be learned anew.

Knowledge of what is does not open the door directly to what should be.

Heroism on command, senseless violence, and all the loathsome nonsense that goes by the name of patriotism - how passionately I hate them!

There is no place in this new kind of physics both for the field and matter, for the field is the only reality.

The really valuable method of thought to arrive at a logically coherent system is intuition.

God doesn't; shoot crap with the universe. Your innermost thoughts are beliefs that unfold as your universe.

In music I do not look for logic. I am quite intuitive on the whole and know no theories. I never like a work if I cannot intuitively grasp its inner unity (architecture).

The pioneers of a warless world are the young men (and women) who refuse military service.

Only strong characters can resist the temptation of superficial analysis.

Time is an illusion.

Formal symbolic representation of qualitative entities is doomed to its rightful place of minor significance in a world where flowers and beautiful women abound.

Keep on sowing your seed, for you never know which will grow - perhaps it all will.

What separates me from most so-called atheists is a feeling of utter humility toward the unattainable secrets of the harmony of the cosmos.

God always takes the simplest way.

Anyone who thinks science is trying to make human life easier or more pleasant is utterly mistaken.

If most of us are ashamed of shabby clothes and shoddy furniture let us be more ashamed of shabby ideas and shoddy philosophies.

The most incomprehensible thing about the world is that it is comprehensible.

Imagination rules the earth

Nothing truly valuable arises from ambition or from a mere sense of duty; it stems rather from love and devotion towards men and towards objective things.

Without deep reflection one knows from daily life that one exists for other people.

It is impossible to get out of a problem by using the same kind of thinking that it took to get into it.

Is it not better for a man to die for a cause in which he believes, such as peace, than to suffer for a cause in which he does not believe, such as war?

I find it difficult to believe that I belong to such an idiotic, rotten species - the species that actually boasts of its freedom of will, heroism on command, senseless violence, and all of the loathsome nonsense that goes by the name of patriotism.

We shall require a substantially new manner of thinking if mankind is to survive.

I like to think the moon is there even if I am not looking at it.

It would be better if you began to teach others only after you yourself have learned something.

I believe the most important mission of the state is to protect the individual and make it possible for him to develop into a creative personality.

The horizon of many people is a circle with a radius of zero. They call this their point of view.

We know nothing at all. All our knowledge is but the knowledge of schoolchildren. The real nature of things we shall never know.

The indifference, callousness and contempt that so many people exhibit toward animals is evil first because it results in great suffering in animals, and second because it results in an incalculably great impoverishment of the human spirit.

What I see in Nature is a magnificent structure that we can comprehend only very imperfectly, and that must fill a thinking person with a feeling of humility. This is a genuinely religious feeling that has nothing to do with mysticism.

After a certain high level of technical skill is achieved science and art tend to coalesce in aesthetics, plasticity, and form. The greatest scientists are artists as well.

Imagination is more valuable than information.

Thank you for your support.

We hope this collection has Inspired You

Humblepics.com